Buddy to School

By Cindy Trumbore
Illustrated by Tracy Mattocks

Scott Foresman
is an imprint of

PEARSON

Glenview, Illinois • Boston, Massachusetts • Chandler, Arizona •
Upper Saddle River, New Jersey

Illustrations
Tracy Mattocks.

Photographs
Every effort has been made to secure permission and provide appropriate credit for photographic material. The publisher deeply regrets any omission and pledges to correct errors called to its attention in subsequent editions.

Unless otherwise acknowledged, all photographs are the property of Pearson Education, Inc.

12 Guang Niu/Staff/Getty Images.

ISBN 13: 978-0-328-51372-7
ISBN 10:   0-328-51372-5

6 7 8 9 10 V0FL 14 13 12 11

It was the first day of Puppy School, and Anna Chen's dog was not exactly the best pupil. First, the owners worked on teaching the dogs to sit. The other dogs began to sit, but Buddy just pulled at his leash and barked.

"What kind of dog is that?" asked the owner of an adorable poodle puppy.

"We don't know," Anna said. "We adopted Buddy from a shelter. My parents said that was a compassionate thing to do."

"Buddy doesn't seem as mature as the other dogs," said the teacher, Matt, to Anna's mom. "Try this. Speak to him calmly and stroke his back. That will help him settle down. When he is calm, he will focus better."

While the other puppies worked on lying down, Anna and her mom spoke calmly to Buddy and petted him. By the end of the class, he sat when Anna gave him the command. Then, he gave Anna a rapid kiss on the nose.

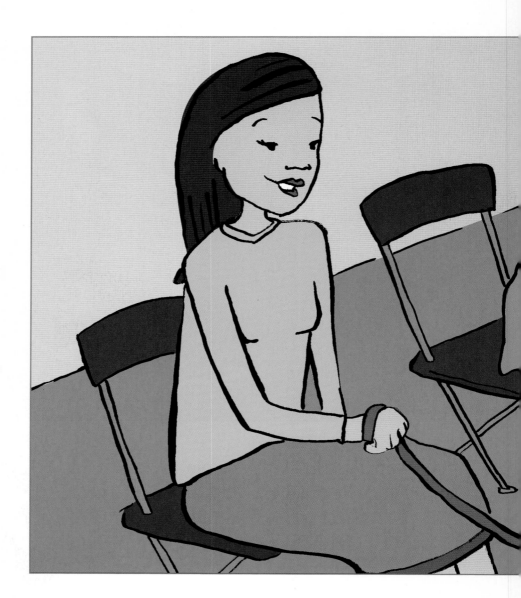

"It is fine if Buddy is not doing what all the other dogs are doing in class," said Matt. "Watch what I do, and then teach Buddy outside of class. Be sure to mention the plan to the rest of the family too."

That week, Anna worked on getting Buddy
to lie down when she said, "Down." Her best
friend, Tia, helped.

"He sure likes to snuggle," said Tia, petting
Buddy. "My iguana doesn't do that!"

At the start of the next class, Matt asked the owners to show how their dogs could sit and lie down. Now Buddy could do both. "Keep up the good work!" Matt called. Anna and her mom smiled and nodded.

During the last class, Matt gave out trophies to the dogs. "Buddy gets the trophy for the hardest worker," he said. "He worked inside *and* outside of class."

Anna hugged Buddy. "I'm so proud of you, Buddy," she told him. "I knew you could finish puppy school. You just did it your own way!"

Dog Training Schools

All over the country, people bring their dogs to dog-training schools. The schools teach owners the commands, hand movements, and praise they can use to get their dogs to obey. Because dogs perform best when they get rewards, the owners bring plenty of dog treats to class.

Some of the classes at dog training schools are just for puppies. The puppies and their owners work on commands such as *Sit, Down, Stay,* and *Here.* The dogs also learn to take treats gently from the owner's hand. The classes are fun for the puppies and their owners.